Advancing Inclusion

Advancing Inclusion

A Guide to Effective Diversity Council and
Employee Resource Group Membership

Deborah L. Plummer

ISBN: 0996672001
ISBN 13: 9780996672009

CONTENTS

INTRODUCTION

Purpose and Objectives

This guide is designed to support your work as a member of your organization's diversity council or employee resource group (ERG) and provides you with some foundational information to understand diversity. It also outlines the process of building successful diversity councils and ERGs at your workplace.

Perhaps when you think of diversity, you think of programs and initiatives in organizations, communities, agencies, and schools. You may associate it with the principle of respect or simply think of it as race relations. You may define it as another term for human differences, such as race, ethnicity, gender, age, sexual orientation, religion, occupational role and status, or mental and physical ability. You may believe that the word has been overused or has a negative emotional connotation and may prefer the term *inclusion* instead.

You would be partially correct with any of these thoughts—the field of diversity is broad and is most often experienced rather than studied as a discipline. The purpose of this guide, therefore, is to introduce you to the basic aspects of diversity and to help you better understand workforce diversity and its implications for you as a member of your diversity council or ERG. Doing the exercises and discussing with your group your responses to the questions presented in the guide will help you gain the knowledge, skills, and abilities needed to build an inclusive organization. Using this short guide, you and your diversity council or ERG will have the opportunity to:

- Unravel the language of diversity and understand its historical underpinnings in the United States

- Understand how diversity helps enhance your organization's mission and further its business objectives
- Develop your cultural competence and enrich your personal development
- Explore frameworks for understanding the many dimensions of human diversity
- Understand the various levels of human systems and how systems thinking helps us understand diversity
- Explore cultural-identity development and the cultural patterns that are part of American society
- Explore how religion and age differences influence work practices
- Understand unconscious bias and its impact on recruitment, retention, and promotion of underrepresented groups
- Gain knowledge of the steps for achieving a successful diversity council or ERG
- Better understand your role as a member of a diversity council or ERG

Although chief diversity officer positions are now the norm in many organizations and departments for diversity and inclusion are no longer unusual, the responsibility of enabling diversity and inclusion in an organization belongs to everyone and not just the diversity and inclusion office or the human resources department. We all have a part to play in building a high-performing, inclusive organization. That is what makes managing diversity exciting and complex to manage at the same time. This guide will support you to understand that complexity, starting with the catalyst for managing diversity, the changing demographic profile of the United States.

PART I: KNOWLEDGE AND SKILLS NECESSARY TO UNDERSTAND DIVERSITY

CHANGING DEMOGRAPHICS

The changing demographics of the United States over the past two decades have greatly influenced how the nation thinks about, works with, and benefits from differences.

How much do you know about the changing demographics that have influenced how you think about and understand diversity? Take the following quiz as an opportunity for learning. Release the need to be right and jot down your first thought as the answer. Your answers will reveal a lot about your perception of the world and your experiences.

DIVERSITY QUIZ

Questions 1-7:
On the basis of the current census data estimates, what percentage (within 3 percentage points) of the total US population does each of the following groups represent?

1. Asians
2. Blacks
3. Hispanics/Latinos
4. American Indians
5. Native Hawaiian/Pacific Islander
6. Whites
7. Individuals with two or more races

Questions 8-12:

What percentage of the total world population lives in each of the following geographic areas?

	A	**B**	**C**	**D**
	Under 10%	**10%–30%**	**30%–50%**	**Over 50%**
8. Africa				
9. Asia				
10. Europe				
11. North America				
12. South America				

Questions 13–16:

What percentage (within 3 percentage points) of the average US wage for White males is earned by the following groups?

13. Black Americans
14. Hispanics/Latinos
15. Asians
16. White females
17. What percentage of working-age women in the United States are presently in the workforce?
    A. 50%–59%
    B. 60%–69%
    C. 70%–79%
    D. 80%–89%
18. What percentage of US families now fit the profile of working father, homemaker mother, and two or more children?
19. What percentage of Americans live below the poverty line?

20. What percentage of the workforce fall under the American Disability Act definition of disability?
21. What percentage of Americans are over sixty-five years old?
22. What percentage of American children are Black, Hispanic/Latin, Native American, or Asian?
23. What percentage of the population is estimated to be gay or lesbian?
24. What percentage of the population is estimated to be transgendered?
25. What is the number of federally recognized Native American tribal units in the United States?
26. What geographic area is the leading source of new-entry US engineers, doctors, and technical workers?
27. What is the fastest growing religion in the world?
28. What is the largest Hispanic group in the United States?
29. What percentage of working-age adults in the United States have college degrees?
30. What is the overall percentage of households in the United States with computers? In the world?

Examine your responses and compare them with the answers provided in the appendix. Were there any surprises for you? What was the source of your answers? Was it your educational experience? Your general reading? What you have seen or heard from the media or general personal experience? Often, when we are unaware of factual knowledge about a topic we rely on, our experiential knowledge to provide us with answers. Because our experience is inherently limiting, we can often be wrong about what we have experienced as truth. Social psychologists call this phenomenon the *availability heuristic*. We draw on what is readily available as truth and generalize this information as knowledge. Examining our assumptions is a helpful skill for discerning whether information that is readily available to us is based on facts rather than perception.

Examining Assumptions

It is probably obvious to most of us that our assumptions play a large role in how we evaluate our environment. Yet this aspect of our thinking often goes unexamined; thus, it is imperative that we examine the underlying assumptions behind our beliefs. By learning to identify our assumptions, we can more effectively explore differences with others and work toward building common ground and consensus. By examining assumptions, we can more creatively and effectively analyze core misunderstandings and cultural clashes.

Go back to your responses for the quiz, and examine the assumptions underlying your thinking that led to your answers. Hopefully, you will have learned more about yourself and your thinking process than you did from whether your responses were right.

For example, the percentages of People of Color in the United States and the differences in wage earnings of People of Color from White Americans often surprise people. Think about how People of Color are often portrayed in the media and in our educational system. When the race of an individual is more often noted by the media when they are a Person of Color, it leads to misconceptions about how racial groups are representative of the total population. The number of Native American tribal units may have also surprised you. Again, think about how we might have obtained this information. In most parts of the United States, information about American Indians is limited and unavailable. Similarly, you may have projected the number of individuals over the age of sixty-five to be much higher than the actual percentage. Again, think about what we hear in the media, especially through advertisements, about the growing population of senior citizens and the concerns of the aged. Commercials for products specifically geared toward seniors are now a regular component of our media experience. Together, all of these pieces of information influence our perception of diversity.

Workplace Diversity Trends

Think about how the changing demographics explored in the quiz—the growing racial/ethnic population, the aging population, the number of women in the workforce. How have these demographics influenced workplace trends? Can you identify what those trends might be? Compare your list to the following:

- Compensation equity across race and gender
- Work flexibility (how work gets done and where it gets done)
- Expression of religion in the workplace
- Diversity of thought tied to innovation
- Thinking and acting from a global perspective
- Technology and its impact on our ways of knowing
- Shift in the meaning of work from "living to work" to "working to live"
- Interaction of five age groups with differing values and attitudes in the workplace:
  - Veterans (b. 1922–1944)
  - Baby Boomers (b. 1945–1964)
  - Generation X (b. 1965–1980)
  - Millennials (b. 1981–1999)
  - Generation Z (b. 2000 to present day)
- The "War for Talent"—recruiting and retaining people with the best skills to meet business objectives and achieve the mission
- Emotional intelligence, including diversity competencies as a necessary competency for workplace success

Thinking about Global Diversity

Managing diversity becomes even more challenging when organizations based in the United States try to implement domestic diversity policies and practices in cultures outside of the country. Gaining conceptual clarity on the definition of diversity and reaching consensus is an important task for any organization, whether it is a mom-and-pop operation or a corporate conglomerate. Working across geographic borders requires getting to know and understand the deep structures of that culture in order to determine what inclusive policies and practices will enhance the mission and achieve the business objectives of the organization. The bottom line is that the United States cannot export diversity; however, it can champion and promote diversity and inclusion within global organizations.

Deborah L. Plummer

In what ways do cultural values influence business practices?
In multinational settings where cultural values are not shared, is it possible for global organizations based in the United States to achieve their business objectives and still practice diversity (e.g., gender equity and LGBT rights)?

Now that we have been introduced to the purpose and objectives of the guide, examined the changing demographics and our assumptions, explored the work trends that have resulted from these demographic changes, and thought a bit about global diversity, let us turn our attention back to unraveling the meaning of the term diversity. Surely, diversity has been with us long before US organizations began to prepare for the changing face of the American workforce. As long as there have been human beings, there has been diversity.

THE LANGUAGE OF DIVERSITY

What comes to your mind when you think of the word *diversity*? Perhaps you think of differences and cultural groups getting along better. Maybe you are focused on race and gender issues and the civil rights movement. You may consider the term *diversity* synonymous with affirmative action or equal opportunity. You may think that it is overused and has a negative connotation. Or that it means certain groups will be criticized and held responsible for discriminatory acts that took place hundreds of years ago. Compliance to diversity principles may be an organization's way of avoiding a lawsuit or appeasing women and people of color. You may find diversity confusing, especially as some people experience religious liberties clashing with the civil rights of gays and lesbian individuals.

Probably, it holds positive connotation for you. You may reflect upon the diversity in your family or in your friendship groups. You might think about a diverse work team that achieved significant results for the organization. You may have experienced that diverse groups are powerful forces that generate new ideas, foster innovation, and advance the business objectives of great institutions.

Whether it holds a positive or negative connotation, *diversity* is clearly an emotionally-loaded term. Its meaning has evolved over the years from its roots in race and gender relations to building inclusive environments and managing basic human differences to being a contributing driver of organizational excellence and innovation. The meaning of diversity is largely dependent on its context. The following sections place diversity in context and define it from the individual (or personal) and organizational perspectives.

Defining Diversity

If you were to conduct an Internet search for a definition of *diversity*, in less than four seconds, you would have over one hundred million results to choose from. The citations would range from topic-related scholarly articles to blog posts by people of all generations and from across the globe.

Diversity encompasses the many dimensions of human differences, including thought and expression. As we work toward understanding diversity in its fullest expression, a growing body of proven methodologies have established it as part of mainstream organizational work and as essential to an organization's success. Several scholarly articles provide evidence for the critical role diversity and inclusion play in our society and particularly in our work environments.

Individual and Personal Diversity

In an individual or a personal context, *diversity* refers to the differences among people with respect to race, ethnicity, culture, gender, gender expression, age, class, mental and physical abilities, sexual orientation, religion, stature, educational level, job role and function, and personality traits. It embraces the many ways in which we are similar to and different from other human beings. As an individual, I am like some people and unlike others. I am unique, yet I am a member of the human race and share other humans' genetic and emotional constitution. That is the *paradox of diversity*. We are unique, and we are the same.

Traditional approaches to understanding differences emerge from a dominance model. This model says that yes, we are all alike, yet some of our inherent differences are considered better than others. Males are better than females, white skin is better than dark skin, able bodies are better than disabled bodies, young is better than old, heterosexual orientation is better than homosexual orientation...and the list could go on for every existing dimension of difference.

You are perhaps reading this and thinking how illogical it even sounds to think that way. Yet we tend to see differences in a hierarchical manner. That is how the brain works. Unfortunately, this kind of thought process leads us to treat differences as independent variables—as if you could go about your day only with your gender or your race or your mental abilities or your age!

Current thinking treats differences from a relational perspective. We, as humans, are a complex intersection of the many dimensions of diversity that make us unique and yet like other people.

Such thinking supports an understanding of the complex interactions of social relations and fosters the skills necessary to navigate our increasingly multicultural world. I cannot separate my gender from my race or my ethnicity, or separate my mental and physical abilities, or separate my age or sexual orientation. I am a wonderfully made complex set of variables that makes me *uniquely me*.

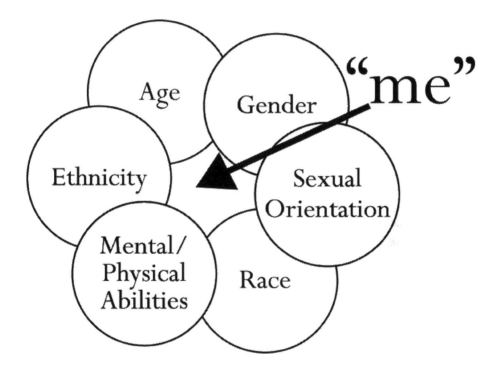

Sometimes the term *diversity* is used interchangeably with other terms such as *multiculturalism* and *race relations*. It is sometimes used as a synonym for *social justice*. Here is a simple glossary of the terms that might help you clarify the meaning of much of the vocabulary in the lexicon of diversity.

Working Definitions

- ☐ **DIVERSITY:** Differences among people with respect to age, class, ethnicity, gender, gender expression, health, physical and mental ability, race, sexual orientation, religion, stature, education level, job level, and function, personality traits, and other human and social differences
- ☐ **CULTURAL DIVERSITY:** Inclusion and acceptance of the unique world views, customs, norms, patterns of behavior, and traditions of many groups of people
- ☐ **"ISMS":** Destructive attitudes or beliefs, such as racism, sexism, heterosexism, ableism, classism, ageism, and other forms of oppression based in power and prejudice about human differences
- ☐ **SOCIAL JUSTICE:** Elimination of oppression and the "isms" to create a full and equal participation of all groups in a society where the distribution of resources is equitable and all members are physically and emotionally safe and secure
- ☐ **PREJUDICE:** Favorable or unfavorable prejudgment of people on the basis of their group membership
- ☐ **PLURALISM:** A culture that incorporates mutual respect, acceptance, teamwork, and productivity among people who are diverse
- ☐ **MULTICULTURALISM:** A pluralistic culture that reflects the interests, contributions, and values of members of diverse groups

You may think that the definition of diversity is too broad to hold any real meaning. Everything about being human seems to be related to diversity. The key to diversity, therefore, is valuing and managing differences in such a way that the results lead to inclusion. The salient characteristics of multiculturalism include respecting and appreciating differences that lead to added value and representation of all cultures. The essence of social justice is to establish fair and equitable systems for multicultural communities and organizations. Here's a simple chart to distinguish diversity from some related terms.

Diversity: Key is inclusion
Multiculturalism: Key is appreciation and respect for cultures
Social Justice: Key is fairness

INDIVIDUAL DIVERSITY

We experience diversity at an individual or a personal level through a developmental process that enables us to express some aspects as core to our identity and others that influence and shape our core but do not fundamentally change who we are and how we understand ourselves. For example, when I was a young adult, race, gender, and religion occupied a considerable portion of my depiction of who I was and how I expressed myself in the world. As I struggled with my issues of racial identity and place in the world as an African American woman, my race and gender became the looking glasses for how I interacted with the world, and religion provided a way to make sense of these issues. Today, as I grow older, age and mental/physical abilities represent a significant portion of my visual representation of my personal diversity identity. As my racial identity and gender role have been defined and stabilized, the developmental tasks of aging have become central to my understanding of the world and my everyday experience.

Young Adult

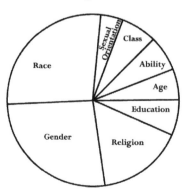

Current

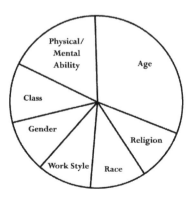

The diagrams compare my past and present circle of diversity. Take a few minutes to depict your representation of the dimensions of diversity in your present life.

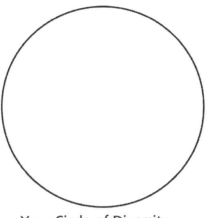

Your Circle of Diversity

Group Membership Identity

As unique as I am as an individual, I also share with others a group member identity. Each individual, too, holds multiple identities. The expression of our identity is contextual and dependent on the level of human system at which our interactions take place. For example, for a Black-American woman traveling in Japan, her identity as an American might be more salient than her race or gender. For a gay man among other male executives, his sexual orientation might be more salient. A female chair of a basic science department might experience acting out her identity as an administrator when she works to implement a new policy, whereas others might give more prominence to her group identity as a woman. Thus, diversity cuts across all levels of human systems and intersects with the multiple identities that an individual possesses.

- **Individual/Intrapsychic:** Boundary is self-system (e.g., thoughts, feelings)

- **Interpersonal:** Boundary with an individual or with a group or sub-group (e.g., connecting with spouse/partner or with a family or with the children of a family)
- **Group:** Boundary is shared identity (e.g., racial identity or nation of origin or religious affiliation)
- **Organizational/Institutional:** Boundary is a systematic set of purposes, rules, practices, and traditions (e.g., work affiliation and religious affiliation)
- **Societal:** Boundaries are many facets of culture (e.g., language, norms, values, sanctions, politics, and acculturation)
- **Global:** Boundary is worldwide (e.g., Facebook, Twitter, Instagram, World Wide Web)

Levels of Human Systems

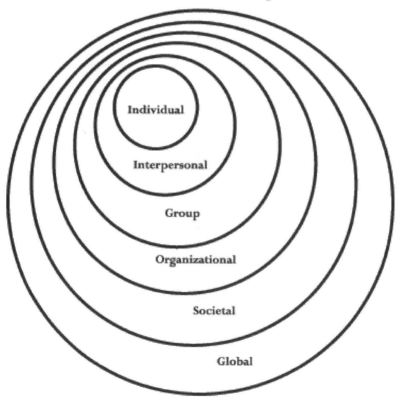

Relevant Terms

Growing up, all of us were embedded and socialized in our cultures. As a result, most of us believe our cultural practices to be the norm for human behavior. For example, when I was a child, my mother exposed me to the Girl Scouts organization. Because I was raised Catholic and attended a predominately White Irish Catholic school, my mother intentionally chose a troop for me that was comprised mostly Black American girls. It was within this context that I learned Negro spirituals. Consequently, I never distinguished those songs from the traditional Girl Scout songs that I had learned. Because our troop leaders, too, did not make any distinction, I assumed all songs I learned in the context of Girl Scouts were "Girl Scouts songs." Imagine my surprise when I found out during a county Girl Scouts summer camp that "Woke Up This Morning" and "Come by Here" were not Girl Scouts songs!

Because of the human socialization process, we are all ethnocentric and culturally myopic to some extent. In addition, the human brain is designed to be reactive to the environment rather than to be proactive and take a reasoned approach. The brain specializes in quick generalizations, not subtle distinctions. We may claim to have no biases or may believe that any prejudices that we might have are under our control, but we all possess unconscious, hardwired processes that do not allow us to behave in egalitarian ways.

We need to widen the lenses through which we see the world and remain culturally sensitive in the process. Following are some definitions of the concepts described in subsequent section:

- [ ] **WORLD VIEW:** An individual's or a group's unique perspective or way of interpreting life's experiences
- [ ] **CULTURAL SENSITIVITY:** Basic and obvious respect for and appreciation of various cultures that may differ from ours
- [ ] **ETHNOCENTRISM:** The tendency to use our group as a norm or standard by which to assess other groups
- [ ] **CULTURAL MYOPIA:** The belief that our culture is appropriate to all situations and relevant to all other individuals

☐ **UNCONSCIOUS BIAS:** Our natural preference for or social categorization of people who look like us, sound like us, and share our same values and beliefs

Managing Ethnocentrism, Cultural Myopia, and Unconscious Bias

No matter how much we value diversity, successfully navigating our increasingly multiracial and multicultural society requires cultural competence. Our brains are hardwired in ways that help us to be efficient and stay safe; however, those same advantages that our brains afford us also present challenges when we encounter differences, particularly those differences associated with negative social loadings grounded in the historical roots of inequality.

Just as we have to work to learn new skills to keep up with technological advancements, we have to do the same to be culturally competent. One of the first steps toward this is to recognize and acknowledge that we are all ethnocentric and culturally myopic in our thinking and that we have biases that shape our interactions with one another.

Acknowledging our ethnocentrism, cultural myopia, and unconscious biases extends beyond the cerebral thought process of just stating, "I own my biases!" Recall that our brains are hardwired to maintain these biases, so we have to do things actively that interrupt our natural inclination to believe that everyone who thinks and acts as we do is right and normal.

Activities sponsored by diversity councils and ERGs are designed to interrupt these natural patterns and build the foundation for leveraging differences in productive and meaningful ways within an organization's structure.

Besides participating in diversity activities and events, you can reduce biases by learning and practicing four diversity competencies:

1. Holding multiple realities, identities, and perspectives
2. Balancing intention and impact

3. Moving from certainty to curiosity
4. Using privilege as a life skill

Diversity Competency #1: Holding Multiple Realities, Identities, and Perspectives

It is necessary to understand the influence of our social group identities (e.g., race, ethnicity, gender, sexual orientation, age, religion/spiritual beliefs, nationality, and other dimensions of diversity) on our thinking and behavior. Because of our brain function and socialization process, we tend to be drawn to experiences and individuals with whom we are familiar.

Just as it can be challenging to see the young and older woman in the preceding image, our ability to shift between our experience and those of others to perceive the multiple realities that exist in a given situation challenges us to broaden our thinking and understand and interact successfully with different cultures. Holding multiple realities, identities, and perspectives helps us mitigate conscious and unconscious biases, eliminate ethnocentrism, and expand our culturally myopic thinking.

Diversity Competency #2: Balancing Intention and Impact

Imagine, for a moment, the following scenarios:

a) A coworker tells you that when waiting in line to process some paperwork at a finance office, she has noticed the Hispanic clerks being very friendly with all the other Hispanic employees. When other Hispanics approach the counter, the clerks laugh, smile, and joke. While all of the joking takes place, no one appears to be working. Your coworker tells you that she is always forced to walk over to the counter to the White clerk, who seems to know how to work and talk at the same time. She wants to say something to the Hispanic clerks, but she knows that bringing the problem to light would force the topic for discussion away from efficiency and toward race. She is not prepared to handle that consequence, so the conversation takes place only among her friends, who are all White. Little does she know that a similar conversation is taking place among her Hispanic coworkers who are just as fed up with the work performance of the two individual clerks, who just happen to be Hispanic.

b) A Muslim woman is admitted to a hospital with acute onset of pelvic pain and bleeding. The hospital is conducting diagnostic tests to determine the treatment course. She has a husband, a father, two brothers, a mother, and a sister—all the first generation in the United States. The family has complained about the floor staff being disrespectful and the dietary department serving "inedible" food. Meanwhile, the husband has been refusing medications on behalf of his wife, and a brother has "assaulted" and "verbally insulted" a number of nurses and aides providing bedside care. The males in the family seem to be making health-care decisions on behalf of a competent patient and are insisting this should continue. Clinicians and caregivers are reluctant, have refused to provide care, and have been slow to answer calls. The patient tells a nurse that she wants the surgery that has been offered, but the male members are rejecting further treatment for her at this time. The nurse gives her a pep talk about empowerment and her rights as a woman and encourages her to sign the forms to have the surgery.

c) A sales executive begins a meeting with a potential client by telling him that he intentionally chose the restaurant because it did not make any reference to the controversial Indian mascot for the local baseball team, which seems to be plastered all over the downtown area. The sales executive thought this introduction would immediately show the potential client that the company was sensitive to the concerns of Native Americans, but from the client's facial expression, it is unclear whether the topic should have even been brought up. When doing a background check, the executive was curious about the client's last name and had made some inquiries. Everyone told him that the surname, Starblanket, was Native American. Now he wonders if the sales executive who had told him that it would be good to kick off the meeting in this manner was just trying to sabotage his success. At any rate, he needs to quickly segue to another topic. So he makes up a story about his daughter writing a paper on the controversy related to sports teams with Native American mascots, claiming that the topic was on his mind because of the dinner conversation he had had with his daughter the previous evening.

d) A young male marketing associate and rising-star performer in a conservative, hierarchical company is slated to receive the company's employee-of-the-year award. During the regular morning one-on-one briefing, his supervisor inquires about the guest he plans to bring to the awards dinner as indicated on the RSVP he received. "Here we were all this time thinking you were so busy with your head down into your work that you had little time for a lady in your life. Well, it looks like the joke is on us," he tells the associate. "You have got to tell me a bit about her," he continues. "After all I will be sitting at your table and will introduce you when you get the award." The associate takes a deep breath and says, "I am happy to tell you about my husband."

e) As a manager, you pride yourself in being able to shape and develop diverse teams that not only achieve results but also exhibit exemplary team work. The daily check-in, where you touch base with each of your direct reports, is part of your routine. In these few minutes, you address questions, offer support, and make small talk to learn more about each of them on a personal level. One day, just before you are about to enter her office, you overhear your best performer, an Asian American, saying on the phone that although she knows she must attend the department holiday dinner, she is tired of the kind of food that is served, the choice of music, and, most of all, the stereotypical remarks made to her that are passed off as "conversation starters." You then recall that just yesterday you talked with her about the new Chinese restaurant that just opened. As you enter, you now wonder if you should begin today's check-in with an apology.

◆ ◆ ◆

In America's increasingly diverse and global workforce and in our society in general, conversations about diversity cannot be avoided. We also cannot afford professionally to have diversity as an elephant in the room during our interactions. As diversity council members and members of ERGs, you serve as role models for communicating effectively across differences.

The following model provides you with a framework for understanding the dynamics of communicating across differences. It lays out a set of skills designed to improve the communication process in a diverse setting.

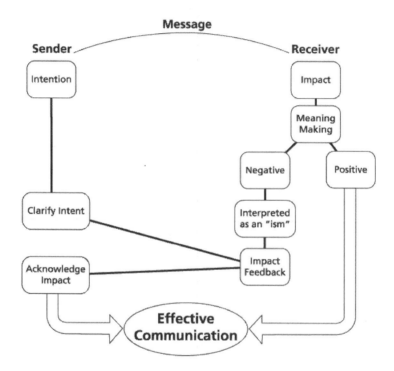

Intention-Impact Model
Communicating Across Differences

Here is how it works:

- The communication process begins with a message.
- The sender delivers a message with a specific neutral intent to the receiver.
- There is intention on the part of the sender.
- There is impact on the part of the receiver.
- Both go through a meaning-making process.

- The sender mentally reviews his or her words to make sure they match the intent of the message.
- The receiver takes in what has just been said and experiences an impact.
- Both make sense of the exchange between them.
- The impact of the message on the receiver may be positive or negative.
- If the impact is felt as positive, then effective communication takes place, and the receiver becomes the sender by returning another message.
- If the impact is negative, then the communication becomes ineffective.
- The impact needs to be shared with the sender.
- The sender needs to acknowledge the impact that the message had on the receiver and then clarify the original intent.

The receiver has a responsibility to inform the sender about the negative impact of the message in a productive manner. Not informing the sender inhibits understanding and can lead to assumptions about the real meaning of the intended message.

Once the sender has been informed, it is important for him or her to acknowledge the impact that the message had on the receiver and then restate the message in a context that better conveys the intent.

While both participants may feel some initial discomfort, talking about the impact opens up the opportunity for clarification and increases understanding. Staying engaged in the conversation is critical to effective communication.

Here are some considerations to keep in mind when practicing this diversity competency.

- ✓ *Intention does not always mitigate impact.* You can have all the good intentions in the world, but it will not lessen the impact of negatively experienced words or behavior. If your actions are not received as intended, look for more effective ways to get your message across that take into consideration how it will be received.
- ✓ *People pay more attention to impact than intentions.* If I wrestle you to the ground and put my foot on your neck and then look lovingly down at you and express my desire to be friends, you might agree…but only on the condition that I take my foot off your neck.

✓ *Language represents your thinking, and words create worlds.* Stereotypes, unconscious biases, faulty heuristics, and fixed mental boxes influence your world views, impact your decisions, and challenge your ability to get along with those different from you. The more you can learn about the relationship of cultural groups with the American dream, the more effectively you can communicate across differences.

✓ *Cultural humility is necessary.* Developing the emotional resilience you need to successfully communicate across differences is a lifelong process. The more multicultural experiences you have and the more diverse the people you interact with, the more diversity competent you will become.

Now take some time to review and discuss the scenarios described at the beginning of this section with members of your diversity council or ERG.

- What are the cultural/communication considerations?
- How do intention and impact come into play?
- What steps should be taken for effective communication?

Diversity Competency #3: Moving from Certainty to Curiosity

If we apply Heisenberg's uncertainty principle from quantum physics to our everyday life experience, we can never be 100% sure about anything. This thought can be both unsettling and comforting—unsettling in that we can never rest assured that anything we do in life is a sure bet, and comforting in that it is so for everyone, and we are not alone in not knowing! We can use this principle when interacting with others, particularly those with group identities different from ours.

Here's a simple exercise to help illustrate this point. The picture that follows has nine human faces embedded in it. It may take you a while to find them, and you might even need support from others in locating them. If you cannot spot all nine faces, it does not mean that the nine faces do not exist.

Similarly, your inability to understand another person's world view doesn't mean it is not real. Denying its existence would be like refusing to accept that there are nine faces, because you could see only five. If the issue or the person is important to you, you might spend more time trying to understand the other person's experience. Just as curiosity may lead you to devote more time to find the nine faces in the picture, staying curious can lead to understanding someone else's reality. Asking questions, listening with the goal of understanding rather than rebutting, and challenging your assumptions are ways in which you can move from certainty to curiosity and expand your world view and increase your diversity competency.

Diversity Competency #4: Using Privilege as a Life Skill

One way to understand the concept of privilege as used in the diversity management context is to do the diversity petal exercise. Here is how the exercise works:

In the flower diagram that follows, write in your characteristic of that particular dimension of diversity on the petals closest to the inner circle labeled ME. For example, for race, I would write *Black or African American* and for gender, *female*. Continue through writing in all of the dimensions until the inner petals display your characteristics of each diversity dimension.

Once you complete the inner petals, arrive at a quick consensus on the "power" characteristic of each dimension with your diversity council or ERG members. By power characteristic, I mean the characteristic that would afford you ease of expression, opportunities, and rights simply because you share that group identity. In other words, life is much easier to navigate because you belong to that group, and being discriminated against because of this characteristic is not of concern.

Once your group reaches consensus on the characteristic, write that characteristic in the outer petal. Do this for each petal, until you have a characteristic for each of the outer petals. Your flower should now have the inner petals completed with your characteristics and the outer petals completed with power characteristics.

In the petals that reflect a match between your characteristic and the power characteristic, place a check. Each check on your petal represents that dimension of diversity where you experience privilege. When I do this exercise with groups, I end up with six checks. There's a match for me in every dimension except race and gender. As a Black woman, I do not share the group identity of a White man (White and male are generally named as the power dimension for race and gender). My characteristics, however, usually match the power characteristics for age, mental/physical ability, sexual orientation, class, education, and religion.

What is privilege? Privilege is what enables you to receive unearned rights, rewards, benefits, access, opportunities, and advantages simply because of your group identity and without regard to achievement. For example, in the mental/physical ability dimension, I experience privilege as a physically able individual who can manage my day without any concern for accessibility. I can go through my day unaware of doorways, hallways, cracks on sidewalks, chair placement, and any number of physical formations that would be obstacles if I were wheelchair bound or had a physical disability.

How does privilege work? Privilege is often experienced unconsciously. It is similar to driving on the same route to the same destination every day. The route becomes so familiar that we become oblivious to the stops and turns. We often get to our destination with little or no memory of the journey. Just as fish in water do not need to understand wetness, when we experience privilege stemming from a group identity, we neither understand what it is like to be someone in the group without privilege nor experience a need to understand it.

When we use privilege as a life skill, we are aware of our privilege and feel a need to understand others who do not share that privilege. We understand that by doing so, we become more culturally competent and effective in our ability to navigate our global society. Using privilege as a life skill is analogous to understanding that a dollar bill has two sides. You know and understand one side of the dollar bill, but also know and understand what is on the other side.

DIVERSITY PETAL

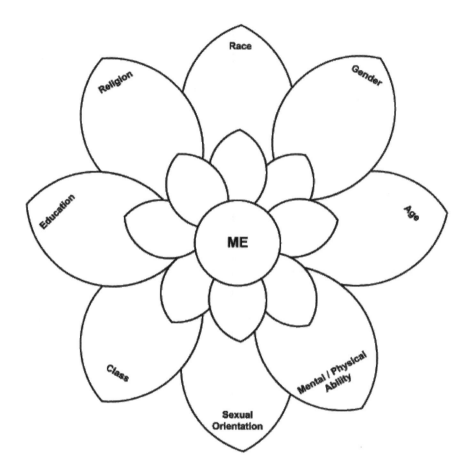

ORGANIZATIONAL DIVERSITY

When organizations became aware of the changing demographics and the cultural and gender differences that would be reflected in the twenty-first-century workforce, many organizational leaders and managers began to examine their workplace profiles and company policies and practices for inclusiveness. Against the backdrop of equal opportunity employment and affirmative action, the notion of fairness and doing what is right motivated many companies to add to their workforce count of women and people from under-represented groups. Other companies realized that unless they matched their demographics to that of the consumers, clients, or patients as well as any constituents they wished to serve, they would suffer as a business or not achieve their mission. Fully functioning organizations have realized that incorporating diversity into the way work gets done and including the different perspectives and thinking that human differences bring will give them a competitive advantage. Progressive companies know that diversity not only makes good business sense but also translates into business cents!

**Fair Organizations → Consumer-Oriented Organizations →
Learning Organizations → Fully Functioning Organizations →
Progressive Organizations**

Diversity at the individual and interpersonal levels focuses on respect and the honoring of differences for healthy personal and professional relationships and peaceful communities. At the organizational level, it is tied to organizational effectiveness, mission achievement, and economic growth.

Employees are considered an organization's greatest asset; thus, it makes intellectual sense to devote financial resources on developing and supporting the people who work for the organization. Although considerable research dating back to the Elton Mayo and the Hawthorne studies reveal that the noneconomic social processes of work are an important contributor to productivity, some organizations disregard or make secondary the social factors of work. From the research on teams and group dynamics, we know that heterogeneous groups often experience decreased cohesion and increased conflict, but once a shared focus is achieved, these groups reflect increased productivity and creativity. Productivity and creativity further increase if the diverse group has the competencies necessary to work together to achieve results. Organizations succeed if they connect diversity to effective practices and support their employees with training to help them become culturally competent and if they have structures that maintain a diversity-affirming environment.

In addition, the buying power of diverse groups continues to escalate, which positions racial minority groups and underrepresented groups as entrepreneurs, job creators, and influencers of the economy. Studies indicate that seventy-five percent of consumers would buy a product from a socially responsible company or would switch retailers if cost and quality were equal. Approximately half of all business travelers are now women. Because of the effects of the global market most American companies have become more competitive in finding and retaining employees. Employees of the new generation bring different and expanded expectations to the workplace, such as a spiritual meaning and a sense of making a contribution to the community. With these facts, it is easy to make the business case for managing diversity, and it would be shortsighted not to manage diversity well.

Defining Organizational Diversity

Diversity from an organizational framework refers to the utilization and leveraging of human differences toward organizational effectiveness and productive business goals. The foundations of organizational diversity are rooted in a clear understanding of the interplay between individual and interpersonal diversity dynamics and social justice issues that are such a large part of the fabric of our society.

For example, there have been several cases where employees have been questioned about the appropriateness of their choice of hairstyle (African American women with braided styles or American Indian men with long ponytails) in the workplace, particularly in companies where profits are tied to selling to the mainstream public. Company policies have leaned toward establishing more conservative or conventional styles—patterned after European Americans—as the norm. The business case from this perspective is clear—if a hairstyle choice negatively impacts customers or elicits even mild curiosity, then it will distract focus from the product or service line and lead to the loss of a sale. The other side of this issue is equally compelling—a hairstyle is a personal preference and not a requirement for selling a product. Americans represent different cultures, and no one cultural preference should rank over another.

What do you think about this issue? How would you handle this diversity dilemma?

Culturally competent companies characterized by learning and organizational effectiveness understand the complexity of this issue. The focus is on what will make the business more effective and what will maintain a high-performing workforce that leverages diversity. To give one side of the issue more weight than the other will lead to imbalance. Resolving this would mean supporting employees who choose to wear a culture-specific hairstyle with the necessary competencies to manage a possible negative response from a customer or even mild curiosity and do the job without offending the client. The organization also needs to support the employee and the consumer with skills to keep the sales focused on the product or service line. Consumers, too, need to be informed about the value your organization places on diversity. Recall that the majority of Americans support and expect social responsibility from companies. When cultural diversity is affirmed in a manner that makes good business sense, it is hard not to support the company's mission and vision, and ultimately buy the product or use its services.

Hopefully, the interplay between individual, interpersonal, and organizational diversity stood out for you in that example. The employee exercises his/her right for a hairstyle preference (individual level), which impacts the employee-client relationship (interpersonal), which in turn may or may not affect a sale and ultimately the bottom line of the company (organizational).

Related Organizational Diversity Terms

In the field of diversity management, some other terms related to organizational effectiveness are frequently used. Knowing these terms will be useful in your understanding of organizational diversity. Progressive organizations have moved beyond equal opportunity employment requirements and matching the demographics of organizations to critical consumers or constituent groups to connecting diversity to organizational effectiveness, enhanced productivity, and innovation.

Following are the definitions of some terms that reflect the proficient incorporation of diversity into the organization's culture:

- ☐ **INCLUSION:** Creating conditions (policies, practices, procedures) that leverage differences to achieve business or mission objectives
- ☐ **LEVERAGING DIVERSITY:** Enhancing organizational effectiveness and performance by using different perspectives, experiences, and abilities that people bring to the workplace
- ☐ **CULTURAL COMPETENCE:** The capacity to function effectively with all cultures and to successfully navigate a multicultural, global society
- ☐ **ORGANIZATIONAL CULTURAL COMPETENCE:** The capacity to function effectively with all cultures and to creatively utilize a diverse workforce for meeting business goals and enhancing performance

THE LANGUAGE OF CULTURE

The terms *culture*, *ethnicity*, *nationality*, and *race* have often been used interchangeably in our everyday speech. Yet, learning the distinct meaning of these terms and using them intentionally in our conversations can increase the effectiveness of cross-cultural and cross-racial communications. Following are some working definitions of these terms:

- ☐ **CULTURE:** A socially transmitted shared design for living and patterns for interpreting reality on the basis of values and practices of a group of people who interact together over time
- ☐ **ETHNICITY:** A group of people related through a common racial, national, tribal, religious, linguistic, or cultural origin
- ☐ **NATIONALITY:** The status of belonging to a particular territory by origin, birth, or naturalization
- ☐ **RACE:** A pseudo-biological system of classifying people on the basis of shared genetic history or physical characteristics

Examine these definitions and see if you can determine the many cultural groups to which you belong, your ethnicity, nationality, and race. As a Black (race), Jamaican/Panamanian (ethnicity) American (nationality), I am aware of the many cultural groups of which I am a part (Catholic, educator, psychologist, middle class, etc.). Culture influences our thinking and behavior in ways that are most likely unconscious. These impacts are transmitted through family, the educational system, and societal practices.

America is host to over three hundred cultures that differ around such issues as control, independence, gender roles, time orientation, and risk behavior. Historically, European American culture has greatly influenced and set the standard for most American norms. Take for example, time orientation. Researchers and philosophers have distinguished between circular time cultures, which experience time as a circle wherein each point in time as sacred and worthy of being experienced fully in the moment, and step-by-step time cultures, which experience time as being composed of the past, present, and future, with attention being given to the future. In some cultures, time is determined by repeated cycles of activities, such as the agricultural cycle of planting, cultivating, and harvesting. From this perspective, time is only viewed in the past and present tense. Because of today's global workforce, which has people from many different cultures, time orientation can present challenges in diverse settings.

For example, if a meeting is scheduled to start at 9:00 a.m., does that mean we begin the agenda promptly at 9:00 a.m., or do we begin to gather in the room and greet one another at 9:00 a.m.? Is the gathering as central to a successful meeting as the prompt attention to the agenda? When would someone be considered late, and what would be the consequences of such behavior?

What do you think? How would you handle time management in a meeting of culturally diverse teams?

Approaches to Managing Culture

Organizations with diverse work environments struggle to manage cultural diversity successfully. With the understanding that enabling individuals to fully express who they are maximizes creativity and productivity, organizations now consider managing diversity to be an essential component of effective strategy and institutional excellence. As mentioned earlier in this guide, managing differences evokes a bit of discomfort individually and interpersonally and, as a consequence, there is discomfort at the organizational level.

Historically, most organizations and community agencies solve the cultural dilemma by adopting one of the following approaches:

1. *Cultural-Deficient Approach:* Popular in the 1960s and 1970s, cultures other than White European were considered to be lacking in cultural strengths; therefore, the best approach to dealing with those who were culturally different was to provide them with opportunities and education for cultural development. This approach is consistent with the melting pot/assimilation model, which was (and, some would argue, still is) dominant in America. Minority populations melted into or assimilated with the majority culture.

2. *Cultural-Blind Approach:* Considered by many to be forward thinking, this approach deemphasizes cultural differences and emphasizes cultural similarity. In theory, this approach appears to be diversity affirming, but in practice, it demonstrates a hierarchical and superior approach. In other words, to deal with differences, the idea is to pretend that the others do not exist.

3. *Cultural-Denial Approach:* This approach also lays emphasis on cultural sameness, but instead of being blind to differences, the existence of differences is ignored. "We are all human beings. We are all Americans. We all put our pants on the same way. We all have red blood inside." Denial of cultural roots, the historical impact for that diversity dimension, and variance in the experience of the American Dream is prevalent in this approach.

4. *Cultural-Tourist Approach:* This approach emphasizes the strengths of each culture and celebrates differences by sharing culture. We "visit" each other's cultures, and are welcome guests. Cultural feasts that facilitate sharing foods and traditions (usually in the form of dance and dress) are popular in organizations and educational settings. Simplistic in its orientation, this approach does not deal with the differences in expression of cultural values and norms that often leads to clashes and miscommunication.

5. *Cultural-Tapestry Approach:* This approach recognizes and celebrates the differences that are evident in multicultural environments. Like an exquisite tapestry that holds individual artistic impressions yet holds a unified art piece in its totality, organizations that abide by this approach

incorporate the various ways of knowing, thinking, and perspectives into the very fabric of how business is done and the mission is achieved.

What approach does your organization use? Are there more effective approaches to take to support your diversity goal?

The "Big Eight" Diversity Dimensions

Diversity management professionals and researchers have found that the following eight dimensions of human diversity are the most often managed for organizational effectiveness in work environments:

1. Race
2. Gender
3. Ethnicity/nationality
4. Organizational role/function
5. Age
6. Sexual orientation
7. Mental/physical ability
8. Religion

Fondly called the "Big Eight" by diversity practitioners, these dimensions have been the subject of intense research on their critical issues. The following chart summarizes these findings:

DIMENSION	CRITICAL ISSUES	INTERVENTION
Race	Communication styles, perceptions/stereotypes, unconscious bias, microinequities, microaggressions, locus of control, career mobility, competitive vs. cooperative behavior, time orientation, partisan politics, philosophical compatibility, loyalty	Diversity awareness and skill-building training, recruitment and retention of diverse employees, multicultural mentoring, group dynamics and team-building sessions, discretionary power mapping

DIMENSION	CRITICAL ISSUES	INTERVENTION
Gender	Communication styles, perceptions/stereotypes, unconscious bias, work-life balance, career mobility, competitive vs. cooperative behavior, partisan politics, loyalty	Diversity awareness and skill training, glass-ceiling audits, cross-gender mentoring
Ethnicity/ Nationality	Communication styles, assimilation vs. acculturation issues, perceptions/stereotypes, career mobility	Mentoring, diversity awareness and skill-building training
Sexual Orientation	Homophobia, sexual double standard, heterosexism, lavender glass ceiling, LGBT elder care, family, adoption	Sexual-orientation education, support and affinity groups, safe-space initiatives, Bring Your Full Self to Work training
Organizational Role/Function	Us vs. Them, communication, values, partisan politics, loyalty	Diversity council/task force, deep-dive sessions, diversity dialogues, town-hall sessions
Mental/ Physical Ability	Socialization, coworker sensitivity, transportation, technical support, career mobility	ADA education, reasonable accommodations, protection from undue hardship, accessibility @ work, technology fairs
Age	Younger: work ethics, values, work-life balance, creativity meaning Older: skill obsolescence, retirement, loyalty, recognition, communication styles	Cross-generational work teams, diversity training, diversity dialogue sessions, technology fairs
Religion	Religious practice during the workday, respect, prejudice, perceptions/stereotypes, religious freedoms	Diversity-awareness training, reasonable accommodations, case-by-case evaluation, interfaith ERG

Understanding Race and Sexual Orientation

Of all of the above dimensions of diversity, arguably the ones most politically and socially loaded are race and sexual orientation. Despite empirical data that support that neither of these is reflected at the genetic level, categorization of race and sexual orientation persists. Since 1960, scientists have adopted a "no-race" position stating that biological variability does not conform to discrete categories labeled as "race." There is simply one race—the human race.

Similarly, several studies have suggested a combination of biological and postnatal factors, but the American Psychological Association has concluded that no findings from any scientific studies have emerged that permit scientists to conclude that sexual orientation is determined by any particular factor or factors. Simply put, we do not know what causes a person to be heterosexual or LGBT.

Why then do racial categories and sexual orientations exist? They remain as social constructs that allow us to organize our thinking about identity and behavior as we experience them. This is why it is imperative that we remain lifelong learners when it comes to understanding people. Our brains are hardwired not to manage differences well. When we experience differences, those areas in our brains designed to analyze and interpret signals are often routed to the emotional section where we are most susceptible to the socialization processes that lead to stereotyping. Left unattended, stereotypes can lead to the perpetuation of destructive beliefs and attitudes.

Let's take a moment to define and differentiate stereotypes from generalizations and cultural patterns.

STEREOTYPES: A widely held belief usually oversimplified and based on limited data and perception
GENERALIZATION: An inference or conclusion derived from empirical data
CULTURAL PATTERNS: Behaviors, attitudes, and beliefs practiced by a critical mass of a cultural group

---

Because these concepts are closely related, it is challenging to understand the difference when experiencing them in your everyday life. For example, a *stereotype* about Asians being conformists may have its roots in the *generalization* of a group preference over an individual one, which is linked to a *cultural pattern* of valuing harmony. Nevertheless, to attach the label of conformist to all Asians would definitely lead to cultural miscommunication and less-than-satisfactory personal and professional relationships.

All of us struggle with fully understanding differences. I have said many times that diversity is a topic I will continue to learn even six months after I am in the grave! Diversity is a dynamic field of study with a history that is now deeply embedded in our societal fabric.

Historical Perspectives of Diversity Management

Knowing the past helps understand the present and better envision the future. The theoretical roots of diversity management lie in the disciplines of business, psychology, education, and anthropology. Heavily influenced by social processes and the spirit and zeitgeist of the times, the field of diversity management has burgeoned since its conception in the 1960s. A brief outline of the historical roots of diversity management that follows will aid in understanding the past and present perspectives. The table depicts some of the highlights of diversity management by decades.

DIVERSITY TIMELINE

1960s

- Origins in Civil Rights Movement
- Overt segregation
- Color and gender blind society
- Social and moral focus
- Researchers note the psychological effects of "isms" on the victim
- Racial and Gender identity development theories established

- Assimilation and acculturation are frameworks for managing differences
- Cultural-deficit models represent thinking

1970s
- Dimensions/frameworks for diversity are established
- Racial and gender differences are the primary dimensions explored
- "Quotas" influence recruitment and retention efforts
- Legal approaches are the drivers for diversity initiatives
- Emphasis on recruitment of women and people of color

1980s
- Values in the workplace begin to be studied
- Hiring/performance/retention practices are examined for diversity
- Social justice becomes the business imperative
- Culturally different models replace deficit models
- Demographic projections in *Workforce 2000* make a business impact

1990s
- Theories of difference are established
- Pluralistic models dominate thinking
- Communications structures that support inclusion are researched and practiced
- Retention issues motivate organizations to be the "employer of choice"
- Organizations incorporate value-added practices
- Learning becomes the model for progressive organizations
- Global issues influence business thought and practice
- Diversity professional organizations begin
- Diversity degree program is established and diversity certification for professionals introduced.

2000s

- Shift in the meaning of work puts more emphasis on inspirational leadership and the people value
- Management models focus on people, purpose, and process rather than structure, strategy, and systems
- Age-related cohort differences challenge the boundaries of the dimensions of diversity
- Psychographics (understanding attitudes, emotions, and values of people) in addition to demographics become business drivers

2010s

- Diversity of thought and expression are considered along with human dimensions of diversity
- Leadership-driven diversity efforts become essential to business strategy
- Diversity is tied to innovation
- Diversity is linked to employee engagement and performance
- Technology tools support building inclusive work environments
- Global reality challenges how the United States exports diversity

How does your organization's timeline align with the diversity timeline? Are you ahead or behind?

PART II: TACTICAL INFORMATION ON CREATING AN EFFECTIVE DIVERSITY COUNCIL AND ERG

ACHIEVING A SUCCESSFUL DIVERSITY COUNCIL

To create inclusive work environments and integrate diversity goals with business strategy, organizations use a specialized group for leadership of its diversity initiatives and to implement its diversity strategy. This group, comprising ten to twenty employees (depending on the organization size), represents a diagonal slice of the organization.

Names for these committees vary and include such titles as diversity council, diversity committee, diversity task force, inclusion and engagement teams, employee engagement group, culture development team, or employee advocacy/affinity groups. Irrespective of the name, these committees are designed to manage diversity by enhancing employee engagement. A successful diversity council possesses the following characteristics:

- It has a clear mission that is tied to the business case for diversity.
- It is accountable for the objectives and has a timetable for the achievement of key action steps.
- It has a link with the relevant management staff. A sponsor or partner from the senior management team is available to guide the council's effort and to demonstrate visible support.
- It selects participants who have the interest as well the skill sets and talent to contribute to the organization in a meaningful way.
- Its participants have broad organizational credibility and are perceived as being objective and results oriented.

- It trains members at an early stage on team building, membership responsibilities, and diversity culture change.
- Its participants seek broad employee input in the nature and severity of issues perceived by employees.
- It employs good measurement tools and quantitative and qualitative measures to enhance credibility and improve the chances of employees accepting resulting initiatives.
- Its activities are designed to connect to the organization's business objectives.
- Its activities are compressed into a tight timeframe to meet the participants' need to see "results" and to help manage employees' expectations of the results.
- It builds procedures for effective meetings—agendas, reports, decision-making principles, and choosing leaderships.
- It sets up a structure for timely replacement of participants.
- It establishes a communication strategy to report efforts to the senior management and the entire organization.

ESTABLISHING EFFECTIVE ERGs

Like diversity councils, employee resource groups, or ERGs, serve as catalysts for transforming an organization's culture into a more inclusive, engaged, and productive one. Employee resource groups are task groups that provide education and bring awareness to the participants and other employees outside of the network. They also offer opportunities for the professional and personal growth of their members. The purpose of all ERGs is to help drive the mission, support the organization's fundamental values, and enhance cultural competence across the organization.

Naming the ERG

The name of the group reflects the purpose, its targeted participants, and the connection to the organization. When naming the group, consider that ERGs are networks or affinity groups that provide an open environment for members. Membership should be open to employees across the system, including those who do not share the group identity of the targeted participants.

Purpose of ERG

The purpose of the group should reflect the following:

- Heightening awareness and educating the institution about workplace trends that impact the group
- Broadening the organizational agenda to include topics that greatly impact the membership group

Deborah L. Plummer

- Developing leadership and support for underrepresented groups within the organization
- Assisting the institution's diversity and inclusion office with recruitment efforts and inclusion programming for members
- Forging effective partnerships in the community and acting as a liaison between the organization and the larger community by extending community service and outreach activities
- Transforming the organizational culture by addressing the following concerns:
  - What work environment conditions or practices help members feel a part of the organization?
  - What can the organization do in partnership with the group to maximize productivity?
  - What can the organization do to maximize customer/client/patient satisfaction and the experience of excellent service with ERG members and those in the community who share the same group identity?
  - What external entities should the organization form relationships with to better understand the needs of participants who share the same group identity?
  - How can the ERG help increase participation in the mission of the organization?

PLANNING PROCESS FOR DIVERSITY COUNCILS AND ERGs

Some of the following suggestions will help ensure that your goals and short-term objectives feed into the institution's long-term strategy for diversity and inclusion:

- Determine two or three goals that can be mapped to the long-term strategy goals for diversity. Achieving more than three goals annually might be a bit ambitious, given that the job you were hired to perform for the organization remains your primary obligation.
- Identify the goals using the SMART model: **S**pecific, **M**easurable, **A**ctionable, **R**ealistic, and **T**imely.
- Identify what resources you will need as a diversity council or ERG member to accomplish these goals. Indicate whether these resources are currently available or need to be requested.
- Identify what support you need from the diversity and inclusion office to accomplish these goals.
- Outline a budget for the year in this plan and submit to the diversity and inclusion office or an appropriate office for approval.

You should design your projects or events to achieve one or more of the following goals:

- Reinforced and enhanced cultural competence (e.g., campus-wide reading of book with diversity-related topic)

- Celebratory nature (e.g., social networking events, work achievement)
- Educational session (e.g., diversity speaker, dialogue sessions, art exhibit)
- Organizational effectiveness (e.g., implementation of process improvement project)

It is awesome to be an effective diversity committee member. It requires continual education and strategic thinking. Many diversity committees and ERGs with no support or training or coaching fall into the "lunch bunch" or take the cultural-tourist approach to diversity as sponsors of celebrations and holiday activities. But even celebrations and holiday activities can be tied to business objectives and the committee's task of enhancing employee engagement. To avoid cultural tourism, ensure each planned celebration has a diversity awareness component that teaches a diversity skill or competency and has a business or mission tie-in.

	AWARENESS	DIVERSITY COMPETENCE	BUSINESS TIE-IN
Martin Luther King Day	Contributions of African Americans to society, importance of community service	Communicating across differences	Buying power in the community, highlighting the organization as a good corporate citizen through community-service activities.
Women's History Month	Gender differences in the workplace	Holding multiple realities and ways of knowing, enhancing emotional intelligence	Recruitment and promotion rate of women in the organization, compensation equity, work-life integration

Hispanic Heritage Month	Contributions of Latino(a)s in the society, understanding equitable use of power	Collaborative conflict management	Business growth in this market
Christmas, Hanukah, Kwanzaa, Ramadan	Religious differences in the workplace, honoring others	Respect and workplace civility	Highlighting the organization's core value and mission
Older Americans Month	Leveraging age differences in the workplace	Collaborative problem solving, inquiry	Valuing traditions of the organizations and institutional memory, understanding organizational culture, employee wellness

To ensure inclusive practices, meeting schedules should take into consideration all work shifts. Attendance, however, should be dictated by never comprising the business objectives of the organization, and the release time for attendance with pay should be set only with manager's approval.

As with all organizational committees, diversity council and ERG membership should be reviewed on an annual basis. Membership is a privilege, not a right. All members should actively participate and contribute to the committee. You may have even signed an agreement with your manager when you began your membership. A written agreement protects the time you will devote to the work of the council or ERG and establishes the work as something important to the institution.

Deborah L. Plummer

Leadership

Members choose the leadership of diversity councils and ERGs. Most often, two co-chairs serve for a one- or two-year period. It is highly recommended that all of the co-chairs meet regularly to share information and create synergy across the ERGs and diversity councils. Quarterly meetings of diversity council and ERG chairs with the diversity and inclusion office or the organization's chief diversity officer are also highly recommended. These meetings serve to

- allow diversity leaders to discuss council and ERG efforts directly with the diversity and inclusion office staff;
- provide time for sharing and discussing ideas, most and least effective efforts, and any topics that need to be included in the organization's newsletter;
- review meeting minutes of councils and ERGs to ensure that the groups' efforts are in alignment with the organization's policies and procedures; and
- provide a vehicle for coordinators and the organization's diversity and inclusion office to remain connected on diversity efforts.

An annual meeting of diversity coordinators and ERGs with senior leadership is highly recommended. This ensures that the system is aligned with consistent communication and direction for diversity goals and creates a forum to discuss diversity-related topics that impact the system.

Executive Sponsors

One best practice for effective ERGs is to have an executive sponsor assist the group in leveraging the organization's brand, build and manage relationships, and enhance visibility and credibility of the group.

Following are the roles of an executive sponsor:

- Attend one or two meetings or ERG-sponsored events a year to make leadership support visible. Have the "answers" at the table, when possible.
- Help align the committee's efforts with the institution's diversity plan.

- Provide feedback to the ERG co-chairs in developing annual goals and committee budget preparation. (Note: ERG budgets should be centralized in the diversity and inclusion office. Executive sponsors are not responsible for supplementing the ERG budget, nor should they be.)
- Report information on the following, periodically and when appropriate:
  - What work environment conditions or practices support the committee to feel engaged?
  - What can the organization do, in partnership with the committee, to maximize employee productivity and engagement?
  - What can the diversity and inclusion office do to maximize satisfaction and engagement among members?
  - What data can be gleaned from this committee to assist in recruitment, retention, and advancement efforts of talented employees, especially those of underrepresented groups?

Communications

Many organizations now produce annual diversity reports that outline the organization's efforts and achievements in advancing diversity goals. This annual report includes a message from the leadership, a snapshot of the workforce's demographic profile, and a summary of the events and activities held that year with program evaluations and any other metrics. A summary of diversity council and ERG initiatives are included in this annual report, but you can also design it as a separate document or web page. What matters is that the work of the diversity council and ERGs becomes widely known throughout the organization.

Your Role as a Diversity Committee or ERG Member

The charge of diversity committees and ERGs will vary, but the following should be your mission:

- Enhance employee engagement.
- Provide good intelligence about the organization's culture and employee satisfaction.

- Identify primary strategic diversity issues.
- Recommend priorities for addressing diversity issues.
- Serve as a good ambassador and champion of the diversity mission and vision.
- Provide ongoing feedback to the senior management team.

Take the time to focus on the following:

- Define the specific gift or contribution that you bring to the organization's diversity council or ERG.
- Describe what diversity means to you and the approach your organization takes to diversity management.
- Articulate your understanding of your organization's business case for diversity.
- Develop the task you are committed to doing in order to help achieve the council's or ERG's goals.
- Incorporate your learning and skill development as a diversity council or ERG member into your annual performance appraisal.

RECOMMENDATIONS FOR FINDING DIVERSITY RESOURCES

Diversity is a dynamic field of study with proven methodologies and success measures. There are numerous resources—far too many to list in this guide—for your continued learning, and to assist you in achieving the goals of your diversity council or ERG. Following are some tips for consideration when choosing appropriate methodologies or finding the best tools to meet your needs:

- Understand what is meant by diversity and inclusion for your organization. A "best practice" only works if it is aligned with your organization's mission and business objectives.

- Change is inherent in diversity management. When it comes to diversity, "If we always do what we've always done, we *won't* always get what we always got." Diversity practices that once worked, even in the recent past, may not be effective when applied to the current situation.

- Ensure that your information sources are not dated. Diversity practices that are evidenced-based and grounded in social science research have a higher probability for success.

- Diversity professional organizations provide valuable resources and the opportunity to network and share information with other diversity council and ERG members. Several reputable organizations exist and can be found by searching the Internet. Review websites to determine if the membership benefits are worth the associated costs for your organization.

CONCLUSION

This guide is intended to support your journey of understanding diversity and to heighten awareness of your own identity as a member of this diverse society and your organization. Understanding yourself and diversity is crucial to developing skills to enhance your personal and professional life. No matter where you are on your diversity journey—just getting started or well down the road—hopefully, these topics have enlightened you and will assist you to be a better member of your organization's diversity council or ERG.

SELECTED BIBLIOGRAPHY

Banaji, M., & Greenwald, A. (2013). *Blindspot: Hidden biases of good people*. NewYork, NY: Delacorte Press.

Jordan, C.G. (2009). Rethinking inclusion: Case studies of identity, integration, and power in professional knowledge work organizations [dissertation]. Cleveland, OH: Case Western Reserve University.

Lieberman, M. (2013). *Social:Why our brains are wired to connect*. New York, NY: Crown Publisher.

Marsh, J., Mendoza-Denton, R. & Smith, J.A. (2010). *Are we born racists? New insights from neuroscience and positive psychology*. Boston: Beacon Press.

Plummer, D. L. (2009). *Racing across the lines: Changing race relations through friendship* (Rev. ed.). Cleveland, OH: Pilgrim Press.

Plummer, D. L. & Jordan, C.G. (2007). Going plaid: Integrating diversity into business strategies, structures and systems. *OD Practitioner*. (39)2.

Plummer, D.L. (2004). Race talk in the workplace: Unraveling intention and impact. *OD Practitioner*. (36)2.

Plummer, D. L. (Ed) (2003). *Handbook of diversity management: Beyond awareness to competency based learning*. Lanham, MD, US: University Press of America. xxvi 609 pp.

Thomas, R.R. (1996). *Redefining diversity*. New York, NY: AMACOM.

Tolbert, M.A. R. (2004). What is gestalt organization & systems development? *OD Practitioner.* (36)4.

Seashore, C.N., Shawver, M.N, Thompson, G. & Mattare, M. (2004). Doing good by who you are: The instrumental self as an agent of change. *OD Practitioner, 36* (3), 42-46.

APPENDIX

Diversity Quiz Answers

These answers are based on the 2015 census data. For current updates, please check the US Census Bureau for information or other reputable sources found on the Internet.

1. 5.3 percent
2. 13.2 percent
3. 17.1 percent
4. 1.2 percent
5. .2 percent
6. 77.7 percent
7. 2.4 percent
8. B
9. D
10. B
11. A
12. A
13. 71 percent
14. 63 percent
15. 101 percent
16. 81 percent
17. A
18. 10 percent
19. 15.4 percent

20. 17.1 percent
21. 14.1 percent
22. 46.6 percent
23. 3.5 percent
24. .03 percent
25. 567
26. Asia
27. Islam
28. Mexican
29. 33 percent
30. In the United States, 84 percent; in the world, not certain. But 28 percent of the world's population does not have access to electricity.